I0818556

DEALING WITH...
THREATS AND VIOLENCE
Mitchell Lane
PUBLISHERS
KELLI HICKS

Parent and Caregiver Tips for Creating Nonfiction Readers

Timely topics in the *Dealing With...* series will interest intermediate and middle school readers and equip them with helpful strategies for coping with difficult situations. Your reader will be introduced to new concepts, facts, ideas, and vocabulary.

Tips for Reading Nonfiction

Talk about Nonfiction

Explain that nonfiction books provide facts about real-world topics. When readers read nonfiction, they gain a rich understanding of the world. They build background knowledge that provides a foundation for learning and academic success.

Look at the Parts

This book contains the following helpful features. Share the purpose of each feature with your reader.

Photos, Captions, and Graphic Aids
The photos, captions, charts, and other graphic aids in nonfiction texts contain a wealth of information. Help your reader identify different ways information can be displayed.

Sidebars
These extra tidbits of information help satisfy readers' curiosity and expand their knowledge.

Table of Contents
Located at the front of the book, this list shows the big ideas within the text and the page numbers where they can be found.

Extension Activities and Additional Resources
A "Your Turn" quiz and "Exploration and Discovery" activities invite readers to apply their new knowledge. Supporting resources are provided in a special "You Are Not Alone" section.

Glossary
Located at the back of the book, the glossary defines key words and phrases that are related to the topic. These words and phrases can be found in the text in **bold** type.

Index
Located at the back of the book, the index is an alphabetical list of topics and the page numbers where they can be found.

With a little help and guidance, your reader will be on their way to enjoying and learning from nonfiction books.

Mitchell Lane
PUBLISHERS

mitchelllanepub.com

2001 SW 31st Avenue
Hallandale, FL 33009

First Edition, 2026.
Author: Kelli Hicks
Designer: Rhea Magaro
Editor: Kim Thompson

Series: Dealing With...
Title: Dealing with Threats and Violence / by Kelli Hicks

Hallandale, FL : Mitchell Lane Publishers, [2026]

Library bound ISBN: 979-8-89260-676-9
eBook ISBN: 979-8-89260-677-6

PHOTO CREDITS
Alamy: Don Tremain, 17; iStock: SDI Productions, 5; pkazmercyk, 6; Shutterstock: Pixel-Shot, cover, 1; Anatoliy Karlyuk, 7; oliveromg, 8; Ground Picture, 9, 32; Lopolo, 10; Pressmaster, 11; Monkey Business Images, 12, 30; WESTOCK PRODUCTIONS, 14; SpeedKingz, 15; samui, 16; ARVD73, 18; Nomad_Soul, 19; Abdallavector, 19; fizkes, 20; S K Chavan, 21; VaLiza, 23; Studio Romantic, 25, 29; PeopleImages.com - Yuri A, 26; Rawpixel.com, 28; Larry St. Pierre, 31; New Africa, 33; ozrimoz, 35; Sascha Burkard, 36; gioele piccinini, 37; Rawpixel.com, 38; Sheila Fitzgerald, 39; Anatoliy Karlyuk, 41; iofoto, 42; Red Fox studio, 44; Longfin Media, 47

Table of Contents

Chapter 1: A Suspicious Situation

Carter

Carter was having a good day. He grabbed his favorite sandwich from the lunch line. He headed to the table where his friends had saved him a seat.

Just then, the adults in the lunchroom started looking at their phones. Their shoulders tensed. One teacher raised her hand. The cafeteria fell silent. "Listen up," the teacher said. "Please quickly and quietly move toward the exit. Proceed outside to the parking lot. This is not a drill. Stay together and stay calm."

Everyone followed the instructions and exited the school. A few kids were laughing, but most had worried looks on their faces. It was clear this was a real emergency. As they huddled outside, students heard the teachers talking about a **suspicious** package that had been found in the building. They feared there was a bomb inside.

Soon, an army of emergency vehicles arrived. There were police squad cars, an ambulance, and a fire truck. Police officers surrounded the building. They moved inside to check out the threat. They searched the entire school. The mysterious package was removed and taken to a safe location.

After what seemed like hours, the students were told that it was safe to go back inside. The search had found nothing. The package did not contain a bomb. It was a false alarm.

What Do You Think?

- How do Carter's feelings about school change? Why?
- How did first responders help at Carter's school?
- What could Carter do to deal with his ongoing fears?
- How do you feel when participating in safety drills at school or in your community?
- Have you encountered threats of violence? How did they affect you?

The rest of the day went on as usual, but everyone seemed shaken. *How could this happen at my school?* Carter wondered. That night, Carter's parents assured him that everything was okay. Carter wasn't so sure. Days passed, but he still didn't feel safe. He couldn't sleep without having nightmares. He picked at his meals. He felt afraid to go to school or even to leave the house. How would Carter ever be able to deal with his fear?

Chapter 2: What Are Violent Threats?

A threat is an indication that something bad might happen. Threats can come from unfortunate circumstances such as dangerous storms or contagious diseases. Threats can also be made on purpose by people who want to **intimidate** or hurt others. Some threats point to real danger. Many others are **unfounded**. All threats cause fear and suspicion.

Violence is the use of physical force to harm, damage, or destroy. Hitting, kicking, shoving, shooting, and bombing are all examples of violence.

A violent threat is an indication that you are in danger of being physically harmed. If someone says they will punch you, they are making a violent threat. Bringing a weapon into a school is a violent threat. Violent threats, and acts of violence, happen to thousands of kids every year.

Types of Threats and Violence

There are many forms of violence. Some are especially threatening to kids.

Bullying

Bullying is common among young people. It is uninvited, **aggressive** action toward a particular person or group. Bullying tends to repeat over time. Bullies are forceful, and their words and behaviors are meant to cause harm. A bully wants to be in control and works hard to make victims feel powerless. Bullies tend to pick on the same people over and over.

Bullies often make violent threats. They may carry out violent attacks by touching victims or their belongings. Bullies might hit, kick, push, or trip. They might steal or break someone's things. A bully's words and actions cause pain and fear.

There IS Good News!

A *bystander* watches bullying and does nothing to stop it. Bystanders are part of the problem. You can choose to be an *upstander* who takes action to help. You can say something like, "I see what you are doing, and it is not okay!" Most of the time, this quickly stops the bully.

Cyberbullying

Cyberbullying happens when a bully uses the internet and social media platforms to make threats or cause harm. Bullies may post hurtful photos, videos, or comments. They may threaten to find and hurt victims in real life.

Online gaming and social media accounts let bullies contact victims 24 hours a day. As a result, victims may not feel safe at home or at school.

Studies Show That...

Cyberbullying is a serious problem.

- More than one-third of all students are the victims of cyberbullying.
- One-fourth of all students admit to being mean to others on social media.
- The majority of people who witness cyberbullying do not take action to stop it.

Fighting with Peers

Some kids use violent threats, or violent acts, as an attempt to settle conflicts. Siblings may kick, slap, or shove each other. At school, a fight may break out in the hallway or lunchroom. Classmates may hold fistfights away from school grounds. Weapons may be involved. These kinds of physical **altercations** are serious forms of violence. They cause emotional **trauma**. They may result in injuries that require medical treatment.

There IS Good News!

You can solve problems with peers without resorting to violence. Use "I" statements to express your feelings. You might say, "I feel frustrated when you call me names. Please stop. I will treat you with respect if you do the same for me."

Fighting among peers is more common in places where young people belong to gangs. A gang is made up of people who spend a lot of time together and who identify themselves by a group name or territory. They are often involved in illegal activities. Gangs can include kids of any age, gender, race, or background.

Did You Know?

Almost all school shooters share plans or make threats before carrying out violent attacks. If you are worried that a peer may become violent, tell a trusted adult right away.

Weapon Use

Weapons used to threaten or carry out violent attacks include knives, guns, bombs, or any objects used to harm others. Gun violence is on the rise. More Americans have access to guns than ever before. Most students who handle a gun get it from a parent, relative, or friend. Students may use weapons to threaten or attack others. They may carry weapons to protect themselves from other students.

Schools want to keep students safe. Some have metal detectors that identify weapons before they enter the building. At many schools, staff members can press special buttons to quickly call for help during an emergency. Students participate in active shooter drills, so they know what to do in case a threat becomes a reality.

Did You Know?

Adults can keep kids safe by storing guns in a lockbox or safe.

Child Abuse

Some threats and attacks against kids happen at home. Parents and other adults can fail to keep kids healthy and safe.

Caregivers can cause emotional harm by yelling, criticizing, and name-calling. They can **neglect** children by not meeting their needs for food, water, shelter, clothing, and medical care. They can cause physical harm through harsh punishments and other types of abuse.

There IS Good News!

In most states, teachers are mandated reporters. The law requires them to contact authorities if they suspect a child is being abused.

Threats, Violence, and the Brain

Threats and violence have a powerful impact on young people's developing brains. Living with constant fear can lead to serious mental health problems like **anxiety**. Kids might become hyper-focused on looking out for danger.

Being exposed to violence causes **stress**. Stress makes a part of your brain called the amygdala jump into action. The amygdala is like a guard, always on the lookout for danger. If it senses a problem, it causes the release of **adrenaline** and **cortisol**. These hormones tell you to get ready for action. They help you react without having to think too much. This response is known as "fight-or-flight" because it can help you escape danger or defend yourself, if needed.

There Is Good News!

Your brain has neuroplasticity. That means it can change as you have new experiences and learn new things. It can recover from damage caused by stress.

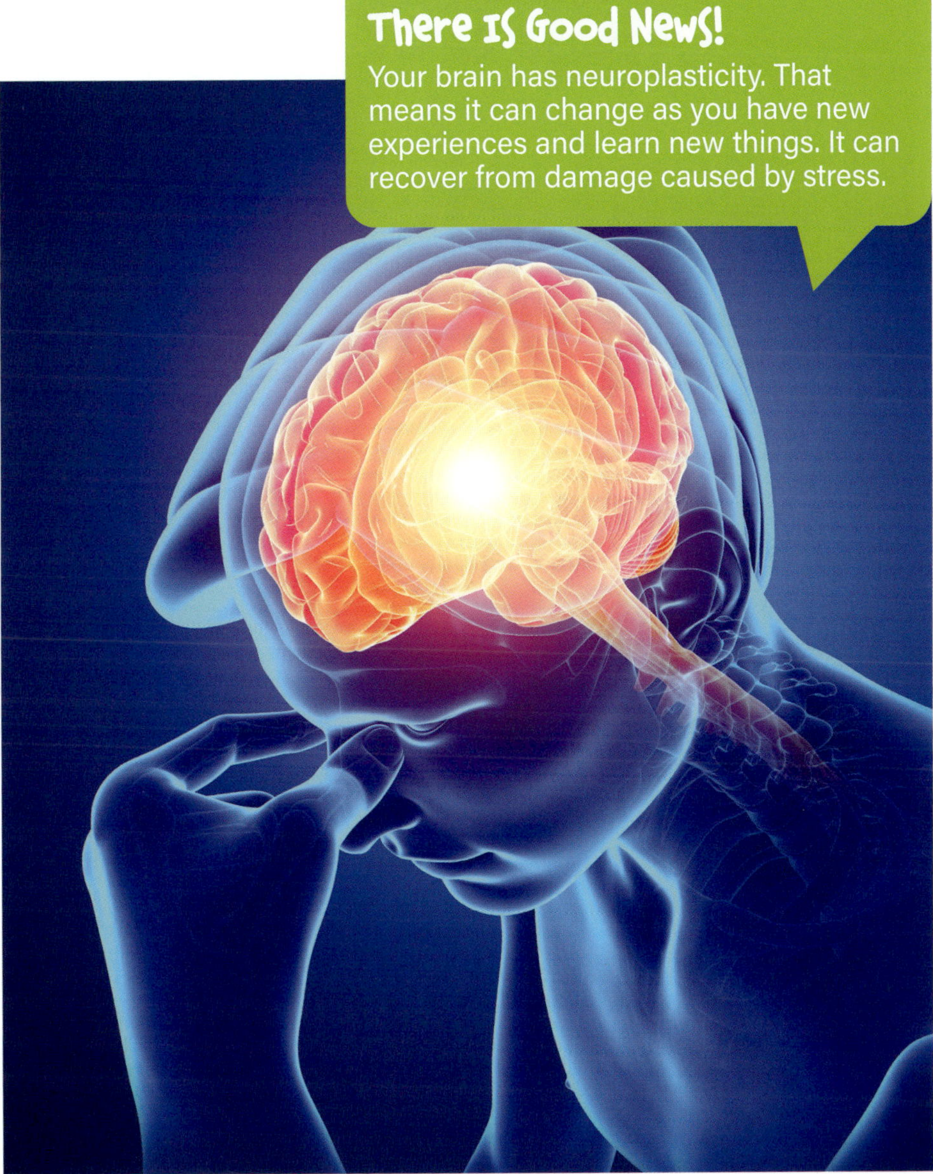

Long-term exposure to stress hormones is bad for your health. It makes you feel tired and unfocused. It can cause stomachaches, headaches, and sore muscles. It can affect your ability to learn, remember, and manage your emotions.

Chapter 3: Effects of Threats and Violence

Being the victim of a violent threat or attack is scary. It can affect you in many ways. It can have serious consequences for your health and well-being.

Is This Normal?

Violent threats and attacks can cause many different feelings and behaviors. The following symptoms are common, especially in the hours and days following an experience with violence.

- **Isolating** yourself from friends or family members
- Becoming quiet around friends, family, and teachers
- Having nightmares or other sleep problems
- Having outbursts of anger
- Starting fights or acting out at home or at school
- Having trouble concentrating

- Not wanting to go to school
- Complaining of physical problems like stomachaches or headaches
- Expressing fears that may seem unreasonable
- Feeling depressed or having thoughts of self-harm
- Feeling guilty
- Feeling numb or emotionally detached
- Doing poorly on schoolwork
- Losing interest in hobbies and other things you usually enjoy

If the threat of violence goes away, these symptoms should also go away in a short time. This is especially true if you have support from caring adults.

Sometimes, the threat continues, or you don't start feeling better. Talk to a trusted adult right away. Living in constant fear is a serious problem. It is never okay.

Threats, Violence, and Individual Differences

Some people have a greater risk of experiencing violence. The following factors make them more likely to be the victim or **perpetrator** of threats and violence.

- ☐ Having past experiences with violence
- ☐ Facing harsh discipline at home
- ☐ Being isolated from others or being the victim of bullying
- ☐ Not having the support of caring adults
- ☐ Being in a gang
- ☐ Using drugs and alcohol or smoking
- ☐ Not caring about school or extracurricular activities
- ☐ Facing **discrimination** because of race, culture, gender, or ability
- ☐ Dealing with depression, anxiety, low self-esteem, or other mental health challenges
- ☐ Having a hard time managing behaviors and emotions

There IS Good News!

Threats and violence are preventable. Many schools have programs to support students who are struggling. They teach students how to manage their feelings and provide resources to keep everyone safe.

Some people have a greater chance of being protected from violent threats and attacks. The following factors make them more likely to avoid experiences with violence.

- ☐ Having strong relationships with caring adults
- ☐ Having strong relationships with peers
- ☐ Being able to discuss problems with caring adults
- ☐ Being part of their communities and cultures
- ☐ Caring about school and extracurricular activities
- ☐ Going to a school that has clear rules and high standards for students
- ☐ Believing that their actions can make a difference and change their situation
- ☐ Being able to manage their behaviors and emotions
- ☐ Having good problem-solving skills
- ☐ Being **optimistic** and having hope for the future

Did You Know?

If you are **resilient**, you are able to bounce back after something bad happens. Resilient people are not born that way. They work to combine their inner strength with good things in their environments. They surround themselves with positive people and ideas.

Chapter 4: Strategies for Taking Control

In many cases, you cannot make violent threats and attacks go away. You cannot control what other people say and do. But you can choose your own thoughts, actions, and values. These strategies can help you feel safer and more in control.

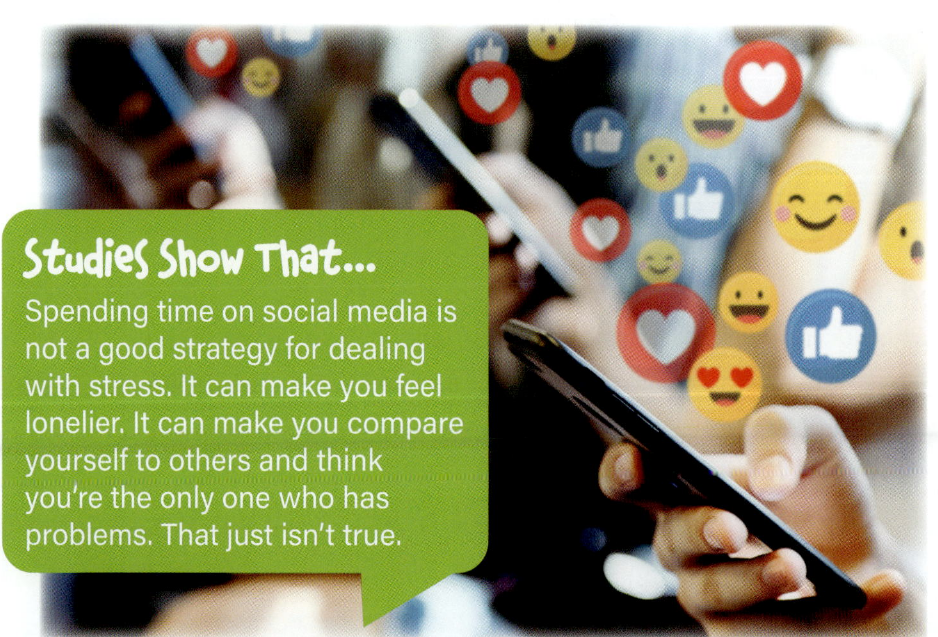

Studies Show That...

Spending time on social media is not a good strategy for dealing with stress. It can make you feel lonelier. It can make you compare yourself to others and think you're the only one who has problems. That just isn't true.

Strategy #1: Build Strong Relationships

Stay connected to people who make you feel safe and happy. Seek out friends you truly admire. Spend time doing activities together or just hanging out. Do not be afraid to share your feelings and talk about your problems. In return, listen to your friends.

Your support network should also include adults who care about you. They can be parents, relatives, neighbors, teachers, coaches, or others. If you are worried or upset, lean on these people. Tell them about your feelings. Let them help you work through problems.

Strategy #2: Get Involved

Preventing violence is a joint effort. Be a part of positive things going on in your school and community. Get involved in clubs, sports teams, and other groups. Encourage friends to join too. Activities like these help people learn to respect each other and get along without violence.

Staying physically active improves your mental and physical health. It helps you manage stress. It takes your mind away from worries and fears.

NFA
17
SHS
14

Strategy #3: Build Your Skills

Learn skills and abilities that will help you become the person you want to be. Be proud that you care about your schoolwork. Whether you play an instrument or play a sport, keep practicing until you master skills that will take you far.

Some of your skills are mental and emotional. You can learn how to reduce stress. You can learn to manage your feelings and solve problems. Practice deep breathing, **mindfulness**, and other techniques. Your school guidance counselor can help you.

Strategy #4: Gain Perspective

Some threats are real, but many are not. Make sure you get information from sources you trust. This will save you from needless worry.

Often, social media and online gaming platforms are not good sources of information. Many hold your attention by making you afraid. They offer only negative or stressful content. They can make you feel like everything is bad. This is not true! There are good things happening all around you.

Block apps that focus on negativity. Take social media breaks and create internet-free zones in your home. When you are online, choose apps that have positive messages. A trusted adult can help you find them.

Strategy #5: Know the Facts

Make sure you understand the real possibilities for violence around you. Know how to recognize danger. Follow these guidelines.

- ☐ If there are guns in the homes of friends and relatives, ask if they are locked up.
- ☐ Notice peers who discuss violence as a solution for problems. Find out which adults at school you need to talk to about threats. If your school has a reporting process, learn it and use it.
- ☐ Know how to report cyberbullying or violent posts on social media platforms.
- ☐ Actively participate during safety drills at school. Know where to find exits and safe places.

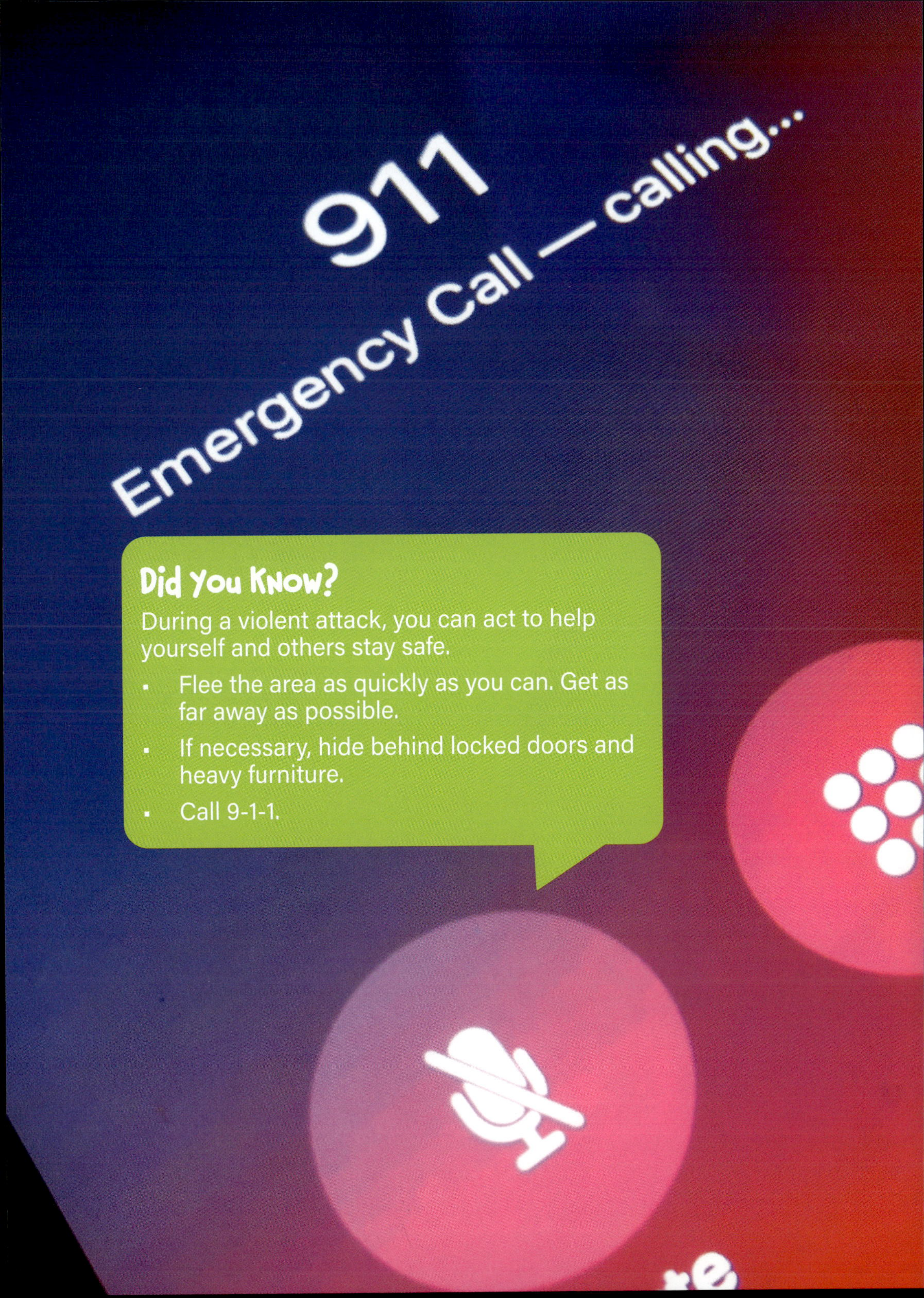

911

Emergency Call — calling...

Did You Know?

During a violent attack, you can act to help yourself and others stay safe.

- Flee the area as quickly as you can. Get as far away as possible.
- If necessary, hide behind locked doors and heavy furniture.
- Call 9-1-1.

Strategy #6: Take Action

Your actions can help prevent violence. If someone talks about harming themselves or others, take it seriously. Tell a trusted adult right away. If you see someone being threatened or attacked, get emergency help. Be strong and speak up! You may save lives.

Be aware of your surroundings. Avoid following the crowd. Do what you know is right! If something feels wrong, trust yourself. Move to a safer place.

You can make a difference in the world by speaking out against violence. Become an **advocate** for victims. Promote kids' right to feel safe. Join an anti-violence organization. Share facts. Work with groups at school and in your community. Get involved in being part of the solution.

Chapter 5: Dealing with Threats and Violence

Remember Carter? For weeks, he struggled to feel safe. He found himself looking everywhere for suspicious packages or backpacks that seemed out of place. Finally, he decided to ask for help.

Carter's parents encouraged him to talk to his school guidance counselor. The counselor listened to Carter's fears. She assured him that he was not in danger. She showed him the school's safety plan for dealing with threats. Carter began to feel a little better.

The counselor told Carter about a new safety group at school. Students in the group would voice their concerns during meetings with the principal and other adults. They would make anti-violence posters and videos. Did Carter want to join? Yes, he did!

Carter knew that the world would never be free of danger. But he was starting to find ways to help himself and others feel safer and happier.

Remember: You have the right to feel safe and to be free from threats and violence. You can learn how to protect yourself and others!

YOUR TURN: HOW DO YOU DEAL WITH THREATS AND VIOLENCE?

For each situation, select the answer most likely to produce the best outcome. Make a note of your answers on a separate sheet of paper.

1. Gavin is new to his school. He has noticed that some kids talk about fighting and wanting to belong to gangs. What should he do?
   - **A.** Avoid the kids that make him anxious. Keep to himself and get home after school as soon as possible.
   - **B.** Try to get to know the kids and make friends with them. They might actually be nice.
   - **C.** Find a club, sports team, or other group to join at his new school.

2. Some kids on Arianna's bus have made fun of her before. Today, one grabbed her notebook and ripped it. Another one pulled her hair. She feels confused and upset. What should she do?
   - **A.** Do breathing exercises to help her calm down and think through her problem. Come up with a plan to ask an adult for help.
   - **B.** Ignore the kids, then go home and have a snack. Tomorrow will be better.
   - **C.** Be mean to the kids. Kick them and grab their jackets.

3. Kids are whispering during Mia's math class. They are saying that a student brought a gun to school. Mia wants to tell someone, but she gets nervous when she talks to adults. What should she do?
   - **A.** Try to find out more information before taking action.
   - **B.** Find the courage to go to the office and make a report about the threat.
   - **C.** Stay away from the student and tell others to stay away too.

4. The chat feed for Colton's favorite first-person shooter video game is full of negative and violent comments. Colton is starting to have bad dreams. What should he do?
   - **A.** Take frequent breaks from online activities. Block comments that make him feel anxious and scared. Find positive things to do in real life.
   - **B.** Respond to the negative comments with anti-violence messages.
   - **C.** Practice mindfulness while playing his video game.

Think about your answers.

1. The best answer is C. By joining extracurricular activities, Gavin can be a positive part of his new school community. It will also help him make friends with people he admires.
2. The best answer is A. Breathing exercises will help Arianna control her emotions and think clearly. She should ask a trusted adult for help.
3. The best answer is B. It is important to take action to prevent violence. Mia should go to a trusted adult to report what she has heard right away.
4. The best answer is A. Taking breaks from being online and blocking violent comments will help Colton gain perspective and have a more positive outlook.

EXPLORATION AND DISCOVERY: ACTIVITIES TO TRY

1. Practice breathing techniques. Sit or lie in a comfortable position. Focus on inhaling through your nose and breathing out through your mouth. Mindful breathing can help you stay calm and reduce stress.
2. Start an anti-violence awareness campaign. Make a social media post or create a poster that gives tips for staying safe in the face of violent threats. Share ideas for dealing with conflicts, reporting threats, and staying calm.
3. Start a Kindness Club at your school or in your community. Support each other and share ways to promote peace. Challenge members to be kind to others every day.
4. Create action plans to use during different types of emergencies. Decide where you will go and how you will contact authorities. Set up a check-in system with family and friends. Create a secret code or signal word to let someone know you need help.

YOU ARE NOT ALONE

Dealing with threats and violence can make you feel hopeless and alone. But you are NOT alone. There are good people who care about you and want to help. There are also many resources you can use to learn more and help yourself.

Explore some of these ways to find the kindness and support you deserve.

People to Ask for Help

☑ guidance counselor
☑ teacher
☑ principal
☑ assistant principal
☑ parent
☑ older sibling
☑ grandparent
☑ aunt or uncle
☑ coach
☑ school secretary
☑ bus driver
☑ religious youth group leader
☑ any friend that you trust
☑ any adult that you trust

Websites

Nemours TeensHealth: Gun Safety

kidshealth.org/en/teens/gun-safety.html
Learn how to stay safe when there are guns around you.

School Safety Is for Everyone!

www.asd.k12.pa.us/apps/video/watch.jsp?v=330633
Watch a video that explains how to stay safe at school.

Stop Bullying on the Spot

www.stopbullying.gov
Learn what you can do to prevent bullying and help victims.

Books

Miller, Crystal Woodman. *A Kids Book about School Shootings*. DK Children, 2025.

Morin, Amy. *13 Things Strong Kids Do: Think Big, Feel Good, Act Brave*. HarperCollins, 2024.

Toner, Jacqueline B. *What to Do When the News Scares You: A Kid's Guide to Understanding Current Events*. Magination Press, 2021.

Phone Helplines

Crisis Text Line

Text HOME to 741741 or message on WhatsApp. Young people of color can text STEVE to 741741 to reach culturally trained counselors.

LGBT National Youth Talkline

1-800-246-7743

National Suicide Prevention Lifeline

1-800-273-8255

Suicide and Crisis Lifeline

Call or text 988.

GLOSSARY

adrenaline (uh-DREN-uh-lin)

A hormone released in your body when you need more energy or when you sense danger

advocate (AD-vuh-kit)

A person who supports an idea, plan, or cause

aggressive (uh-GRES-iv)

Showing fierce or threatening behavior

altercations (awl-tur-KAY-shuhnz)

Loud fights or disagreements, especially those that happen in public

anxiety (ang-ZYE-i-tee)

Feelings of worry or fear

cortisol (KOR-tuh-suhl)

A hormone produced by the adrenal glands when the body is under stress

discrimination (dis-krim-i-NAY-shuhn)

Unfair treatment of someone because they are different

homicide (HAH-mi-side)

The crime of killing someone; murder

intimidate (in-TIM-i-date)

To frighten someone, especially in order to make them do something

isolating (EYE-suh-lay-ting)
Staying away from other people

mindfulness (MINDE-fuhl-nis)
The practice of focusing your attention on the present moment

neglect (ni-GLEKT)
Failure to take care of someone or something

optimistic (ahp-tuh-MIS-tik)
Believing that things will turn out well; positive

perpetrator (PUR-puh-tray-tur)
Someone who commits a crime or other offense

resilient (ri-ZIL-yuhnt)
Able to recover from bad things that happen or to adjust to changes; being strong during tough times

stress (stres)
Worry, strain, or pressure

suspicious (suh-SPISH-uhs)
Giving the impression that something is wrong, untrustworthy, or dangerous

trauma (TRAW-muh)
A severe and painful emotional shock

unfounded (uhn-FOUN-duhd)
Baseless; not true or valid

INDEX

ABOUT THE AUTHOR

Kelli Hicks is a teacher, mom, and author who lives in Tampa, Florida. She tries her best to help her students, and her own kids, understand how important it is to be safe. Constant access to social media and the pressures to fit in can be overwhelming and contribute to violent threats. Kelli advocates for safety and makes sure she understands the safety policies at every school she visits.